W9-AQB-317

PENGUINS

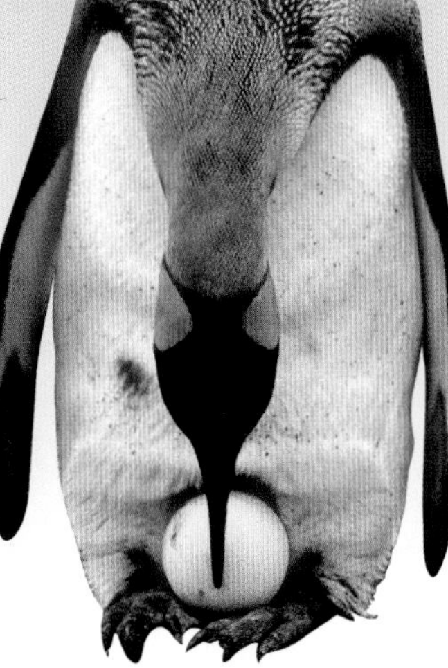

by Lucia Raatma

Children's Press®

An Imprint of Scholastic Inc.
New York Toronto London Auckland Sydney
Mexico City New Delhi Hong Kong
Danbury, Connecticut

Content Consultant
Dr. Stephen S. Ditchkoff
Professor of Wildlife Sciencies
Auburn University
Auburn, Alabama

Photographs © 2012: age fotostock/E Hummel: 4, 5 background, 19; Alamy Images: 11 (Enrique R. Aguirre Aves), 32, 33 (Juniors Bildarchiv), 39 (Mike Lawrance 03); AP Images/John Hrusa/IFAW: 34, 35; Bob Italiano: 44 foreground, 45 foreground; Dreamstime: 1, 3 foreground, 23 (Adeliepenguin), 2, 3 background, 44 background, 45 background (Antoine Beyeler), cover (boboling), 12, 13 (Musat), 24, 25 (Photodynamic); Getty Images/Keren Su: 28, 29; Landov/Mike Greenlar/The Post-Standard: 5 bottom, 40, 41; Photo Researchers/Jaime Chirinos: 31; Shutterstock, Inc.: 8 (Jan Martin Will), 5 top, 27 (Leksele); Superstock: 20, 21 (age fotostock), 15 (Minden Pictures), 6, 7, 16 (NHPA), 36 (Wolfgang Kaehler).

Library of Congress Cataloging-in-Publication Data
Raatma, Lucia.
Penguins/by Lucia Raatma.
p. cm.–(Nature's children)
Includes bibliographical references and index.
ISBN-13: 978-0-531-20906-6 (lib. bdg.)
ISBN-10: 0-531-20906-7 (lib. bdg.)
ISBN-13: 978-0-531-21081-9 (pbk.)
ISBN-10: 0-531-21081-2 (pbk.)
1. Penguins–Juvenile literature. I. Title. II. Series.
QL696.S473R335 2012
598.47–dc23 2011031075

Printed in China 62

1 2 3 4 5 6 7 8 9 10 R 21 20 19 18 17 16 15 14 13 12

FACT FILE

Penguins

Class	Aves
Order	Sphenisciformes
Family	Spheniscidae
Genus and Species	Most scientists agree that there are currently 18 species of penguins
World distribution	All 18 species of penguin are found in the Southern Hemisphere; most are located on islands just north of Antarctica
Habitats	Cold, icy areas; tropical islands
Distinctive physical characteristics	All adult penguins are covered in feathers; most are black on their backs and white on their undersides; long bodies, large heads, and short necks; wings are similar to flippers; webbed feet
Habits	Very social; most live in large groups
Diet	Most eat seafood such as fish, krill, and squid

PENGUINS

Contents

CHAPTER 1

All About Penguins

Penguins are a type of bird. But they do not fly. Instead, they use their wings as flippers. That makes penguins strong swimmers. Penguins' feathers are different from those of most other birds. They are short, thick, and shiny. They also lock together to keep water from getting to the penguins' skin. These feathers give penguins their famous black-and-white markings.

Most scientists agree that there are 18 different species. Each species is different from the others in certain ways. King penguins have orange patches on the sides of their heads and across their chests. Chinstrap penguins have a thin, black line running under their chins. Rockhopper and macaroni penguins have crests of orange or yellow feathers. These appear above their eyes and along the sides of their heads.

Male and female penguins look alike. Baby penguins have fluffy, gray feathers when they are born. It takes time for a chick to get the markings of an adult.

With their crests of yellow feathers, red eyes, and pink feet, rockhoppers stand out from other penguin species.

Penguin Basics

The largest type of penguin is the emperor. Emperor penguins can weigh 75 pounds (34 kilograms) and be 3.5 feet (1 meter) tall. The smallest type of penguin is the little penguin. Littles weigh about 2 pounds (1 kg) and are just 16 inches (41 centimeters) tall.

Penguins live in areas in the **Southern Hemisphere**, which is below the **equator**. Emperor and Adélie penguins live in Antarctica. But not all penguins live in a cold **habitat**. African penguins live in South Africa. Humboldt penguins live in Peru and Chile. Others live in Australia and New Zealand. Galápagos penguins live on the Galápagos Islands.

Most penguins can live to be 15 to 20 years old. But many penguins may die earlier than that. Some penguins starve in cold winter conditions. Others are killed and eaten by **predators**.

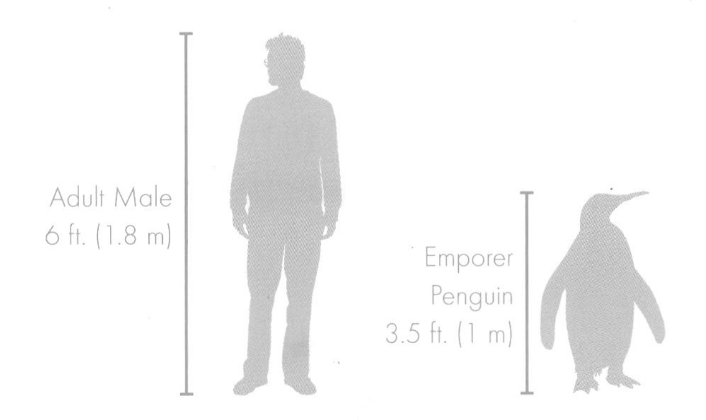

Emperor penguins have yellow patches on the sides of their necks.

CHAPTER 2

Staying Alive

Many penguins live where it is very cold. These penguins have a layer of fat just below the surface of the skin that helps keep them from freezing. There are layers of feathers on top of the fat and skin. These feathers overlap, which also helps to keep the penguins warm. Like many birds, penguins have a special gland that produces oil. Penguins use their beaks to rub this oil on their feathers. This helps protect them from wind and water.

Penguins that live in Antarctica and other cold places huddle together. They stand shoulder to shoulder. This allows them to share their warmth.

Other penguins live in places where the weather gets hot. They work to stay cool. Galápagos penguins fluff their feathers and spread their wings out wide to cool off.

All penguins are **warm-blooded**, just like other birds. Their regular body temperature is around 100 degrees Fahrenheit (38 degrees Celsius).

Penguins use their beaks to keep their feathers clean and oiled.

Excellent Fishers

Most penguins live near water. Their main food source is fish. They also eat **krill**, squid, and **crustaceans**. Penguins spend a great deal of time swimming to catch food. They cannot breathe underwater. But many species can hold their breath for several minutes.

Most penguins dive deep underwater to feed. Many go as far as 60 feet (18 m) below the surface. They rely on their excellent eyesight to see and catch food. Penguins use their sharp bills for grabbing fish. Their jaws are very strong. Penguins swallow their food whole and keep swimming.

Penguins also have short spikes that face backward on their tongues. These help penguins hold on to fish they have caught. Penguins drink saltwater. They have special **glands** in their bodies that **filter** the salt out and push it through their nasal passages.

Penguins have clear eyelids that they use as goggles when they dive underwater.

Penguins on the Move

Penguins have long bodies and webbed feet. Their short legs are set far back on their bodies. This makes them stand upright on land. They use short steps and hops when they walk.

When penguins swim, they use their wings for speed and direction. The motion of their wings makes them look like they are flying underwater. Short legs and webbed feet also help penguins to swim.

A penguin's bill is important for **preening**. Preening is the way they groom their feathers. Penguins have to preen to keep their feathers in good condition. This ensures that the feathers provide protection and remain waterproof when they swim.

Penguins also **toboggan** to slide across the ice!

Penguins can jump about 6 feet (1.8 m) into the air.

Penguins and Their Predators

Penguins face many dangers in the wild. They must watch out for a number of predators when they are in the water. These include leopard seals, sharks, sea lions, and killer whales.

The penguins' black-and-white markings help them survive. Their black backs blend in to the dark surface of the ocean when viewed from above. Their white undersides blend in to the lighter surface of the water when seen from below.

On land, penguins face predators such as foxes, lizards, rats, and snakes. Weasels, wild dogs, and other birds often feed on penguin eggs. Larger birds may also attack young chicks that wander away from the group. Penguins have few defenses from predators on land, so they try to stick together in large groups.

Other birds sometimes try to steal eggs or chicks from penguin nests.

CHAPTER 3

Life in a Penguin Colony

Most penguins live in large colonies. They often swim and feed in groups. Communication in these crowded groups is very important to penguin life. All penguins in a colony look almost exactly the same. Their sounds help them tell each other apart. Each penguin sounds a little different from the others. Male penguins also sound different from female penguins. This helps the penguins as they look for mates.

Penguins also make sounds to signal danger. When they see a predator, they make a special threat call. This call lets all nearby penguins know there is a threat in the area.

In addition to making sounds, penguins communicate by head and flipper waving, bowing, and other gestures. Sometimes they also preen each other. This is a sign of friendship.

Female penguins choose which males they will mate with.

Building Nests

Penguins gather in a nesting area called a rookery when they mate. Different penguins build different nests depending on where they live. Magellanic penguins build their nests underground. They burrow in a way similar to gophers. Northern and southern rockhopper penguins make their homes on rocky hillsides. Chinstrap penguins make their nests out of rocks and stones.

Emperor and king penguins do not make nests like other penguins. They march for miles and miles from the sea to a mating area. Emperor penguins gather on wide surfaces of ice. King penguins stay in groups on beaches, away from snow and ice.

Most penguins stay together for the rest of their lives after mating. But some penguins will choose other mates from year to year. This usually happens if a male does not return to the rookery the next year. It may also happen if the pair did not produce a chick.

Some penguins gather grass and sticks to use to build their nests.

Penguin Parents

Most types of penguins produce two eggs at a time. Often, only one of the two chicks will survive. A nest of eggs is called a **clutch**. Emperor and king penguins have just one egg each mating season.

Female penguins leave to find food for themselves after the eggs are laid. The males are left behind to care for the eggs. This is especially challenging for emperor and king penguins. They live in very cold areas. They have to keep the eggs warm. The male penguin stands and keeps the egg on a **brood patch**. This is a section of skin above the male penguin's feet. This area is very warm and helps the egg **incubate**.

Some penguin eggs incubate in just a month. Others take more than two months. This can be an especially difficult time for emperor penguins in the extreme cold. In most species, the male and female share incubation duties. They trade off every few days. Emperor penguins are slightly different. Female emperor penguins may leave for weeks. The male penguins have no food to eat during this entire time.

Extra blood flows to the brood patch to produce heat.

Feeding and Caring for Chicks

Female emperor penguins often don't return to their eggs until the chicks are about to hatch. The male penguin leaves to feed once the female is back.

Both male and female penguins **regurgitate** their food to feed their chicks. This means that they bring food they have already eaten back up their throats. The penguin parent opens its mouth and leans over. The chick reaches up to feed from its parent's mouth.

Caring for chicks is difficult work for parent penguins. Chicks can die from the cold. Other animals may eat the chicks if they stray from the group. Luckily, each chick has a unique call that its parents recognize. This makes it easier for the mom and dad to find the chick if it is lost or in danger.

Many penguin chicks starve to death before they are a year old.

Penguin Chicks Grow Up

Penguins have soft feathers that are not waterproof when they are first born. They have to stay out of the sea until adult feathers grow in. For Adélie penguins, it takes several weeks for adult feathers to develop. It can take as long as 13 months for these feathers to develop for king penguins. Penguins learn to swim and feed with their parents once they grow waterproof feathers. Then they become independent.

Most penguins are ready to mate when they are around five years old. Some are ready earlier. Others take longer. Then they begin the cycle of life all over again.

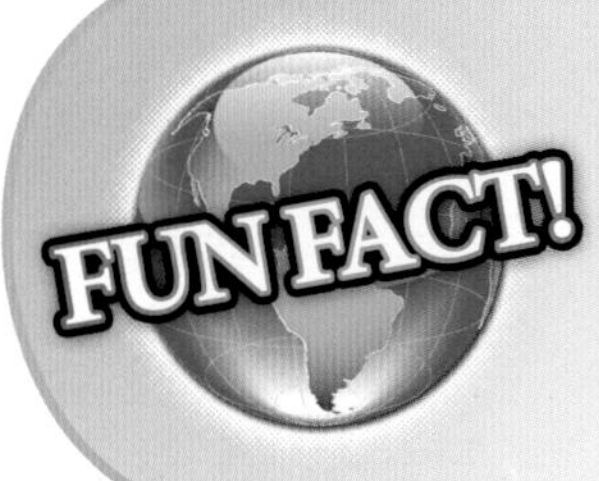

When huddling together, penguins take turns being at the warm center of the group.

A penguin's waterproof feathers grow in little by little.

CHAPTER 4

Penguins of the Past

Scientists believe that penguins have been on Earth for millions of years. The oldest penguin **fossils** date back some 60 million years. Scientists believe that penguin flippers used to be flying wings. These wings became needed for swimming instead of flying as the penguins changed over time.

There once may have been more than 40 species of penguins. Many of those species are now **extinct**. The great auk is also extinct. It looked a lot like a penguin and also did not fly. Scientists once thought the two birds were related. But they know now that the species are actually not related. Today's penguins are related to petrels, seagulls, and albatrosses.

Scientists learn about penguins by studying how they behave in the wild.

Penguin Fossil Finds

Penguin fossils have been found in New Zealand, Australia, Argentina, and South Africa. Only a small number of fossils have been found in Antarctica. This makes scientists think that penguins first lived in warmer areas. Then they migrated to Antarctica.

Most penguin fossils are not complete skeletons. They are just small parts of penguin bodies. Researchers have found bones from feet, heads, and flippers. Scientists have learned a great deal about penguins by gathering fossils. Two extinct species called *Anthropornis nordenskjoeldi* and *Pachydyptes ponderosus* were nearly 6 feet (1.8 m) tall. That is as tall as an adult human.

Penguins can stay underwater for more than 20 minutes at a time.

This painting shows that some penguin ancestors had long, pointed bills.

Discovering Penguins

Many explorers took to the sea in the 1400s to sail around the world. They are among the first modern people to ever see penguins. Some saw the birds near the Cape of Good Hope in Africa. Others saw the birds on the shores of Peru. They drew pictures and wrote down descriptions of the birds. The penguins were unlike any other birds these men had seen before.

The explorers killed the penguins for food. They noted that the birds were easy to catch because they could not run fast or fly. Sir Francis Drake recorded seeing penguins in the 1500s. These were likely Magellanic penguins. Some people say that Magellanic penguins are named for the explorer Ferdinand Magellan. Other people say that they are named for the Straits of Magellan where they live.

The name *penguin* was first used in 1588. One theory about its origin is that the word comes from a Welsh phrase, *pen gwyn*. It means "white head."

Penguins were often killed for their oil during the 1800s. The oil was used for lighting and fuel. People also ate penguin eggs.

Magellanic penguins were likely the species witnessed by Sir Francis Drake.

CHAPTER 5

Today and Tomorrow

Penguins rely on the sea for food. So penguins are in danger when oceans are threatened. Today, oceans are harmed by pollution. Chemicals and trash are often dumped into the water. This kills the fish that penguins need to survive. It can also make the fish poisonous for the penguins. Penguins also are injured and killed when they eat trash that has been tossed into the water.

Penguins are affected when oil tankers accidentally spill oil in the sea. The oil prevents the penguins' feathers from being waterproof. This means that they can no longer stay warm when they swim. The oil also destroys fish and krill that the penguins need for food.

Humans catch fish to sell and eat. Some oceans are overfished. This means that few fish are left behind for other animals to eat. Some penguins may starve because of overfishing.

It is very difficult for penguins to clean spilled oil from their feathers.

Human Problems

Human activity has destroyed many penguin colonies. This happens when natural areas are cleared to build roads and construct buildings. Tourists may sometimes damage penguin colonies as well. Their airplanes may fly too low or get too close to the birds. Humans have also introduced some predators to penguin habitats. These include rats, dogs, and pigs.

It is now illegal to steal penguin eggs or to hunt penguins. But people continue these practices in some areas of the world.

Guano is penguin waste matter. It has been used as fertilizer for hundreds of years. Sometimes people disturb penguin nests when they gather the guano. This practice has harmed the Humboldt penguins most of all.

Penguins sometimes wander into towns in countries such as South Africa.

Wild Weather

Earth's climate changes slowly as time passes. Temperatures around the world have been on the rise in recent years. This can cause ice to melt, which damages the penguins' habitat in Antarctica. Warmer weather also has an impact on penguins in tropical areas. These penguins may get so hot that they cannot cool off completely.

El Niño is a weather event that has hurt penguins. El Niño is a change in water currents and winds in the Pacific Ocean. This change occurs naturally, but it warms the water and affects its nutrients. El Niño can kill krill and other small fish. This hurts the penguins' food supply. In 1982, El Niño caused more than half of the Humboldt penguins in Peru to die. It also destroyed nearly three-quarters of the Galápagos penguins.

El Niño is one of the reasons that the Humboldt penguin is an endangered species today.

Protecting Penguins

Today, the Galápagos penguin is considered endangered. This means that it is at risk of dying off. A few other species are considered threatened. Scientists and other wildlife professionals are working to protect penguins. They promote the conservation of the penguins' habitats. They urge people to keep oceans and seas clean and safe.

Few people see penguins in the wild. Instead, they see them at zoos throughout the world. Many zoos are careful to provide penguins with large enclosures. They try to make their zoo homes similar to their natural habitat. People can learn about penguins' habits and behaviors at zoos. This knowledge may help encourage the protection and conservation of penguins all over the globe.

Zoos work to increase penguin populations by studying them and breeding them in captivity.

Words to Know

brood patch (BROOD PATCH) — an area of skin on which an egg is kept warm

chick (CHIK) — a very young bird

climate (KLYE-mit) — the weather typical of a place over a long period of time

clutch (KLUHCH) — a nest of eggs

colonies (KAH-luh-neez) — large groups of animals that live together

conservation (kon-sur-VAY-shun) — the act of protecting an environment and the living things in it

crustaceans (krus-TAY-shunz) — animals such as shrimp, crabs, lobsters, and crayfish that have jointed legs, hard shells, and no backbones

El Niño (EL NEE-nyo) — a natural change in the wind and ocean currents in an area of the Pacific Ocean

endangered (en-DAYN-jurd) — at risk of becoming extinct, usually because of human activity

equator (i-KWAY-tur) — an imaginary line around the middle of Earth that is an equal distance from the North and South Poles

extinct (ik-STINGKT) — no longer found alive

fertilizer (FUR-tuh-lize-ur) — a substance put into soil to help plants grow better

filter (FIL-tur) — to clean by separating out harmful material

fossils (FOSS-uhlz) — the hardened remains of prehistoric plants and animals

glands (GLANDZ) — organs in the body that produce natural chemicals

guano (GWAH-noh) — dried waste matter of birds that is used as fertilizer

habitat (HAB-uh-tat) — the place where an animal or a plant is usually found

incubate (ING-kyuh-bate) — to keep eggs warm before they hatch

krill (KRIL) — tiny shrimplike sea creatures

mates (MAYTZ) — animals that join together to reproduce

migrated (MY-grayt-id) — moved from one area to another

predators (PREH-duh-turz) — animals that live by hunting other animals for food

preening (PREEN-ing) — the act of cleaning and arranging feathers with the bill

regurgitate (ri-GUR-ji-tate) — to bring food from the stomach back up to the mouth

rookery (RUK-ur-ee) — a place where birds give birth to young

Southern Hemisphere (SUHTH-urn HEM-i-sfeer) — the half of Earth that is below the equator

species (SPEE-sheez) — one of the groups into which animals and plants of the same genus are divided

threatened (THRET-uhnd) — at risk of becoming endangered

toboggan (tuh-BAH-guhn) — for a penguin, to slide on its underside, as if on a sled

warm-blooded (WORM-BLUHD-id) — describing animals whose body temperature stays about the same, even if the temperature around them is very hot or very cold

NORTH
AMERICA
PACIFIC
OCEAN
ATLANTIC
SOUTH
AMERICA
Galápagos Penguin
Penguin Range

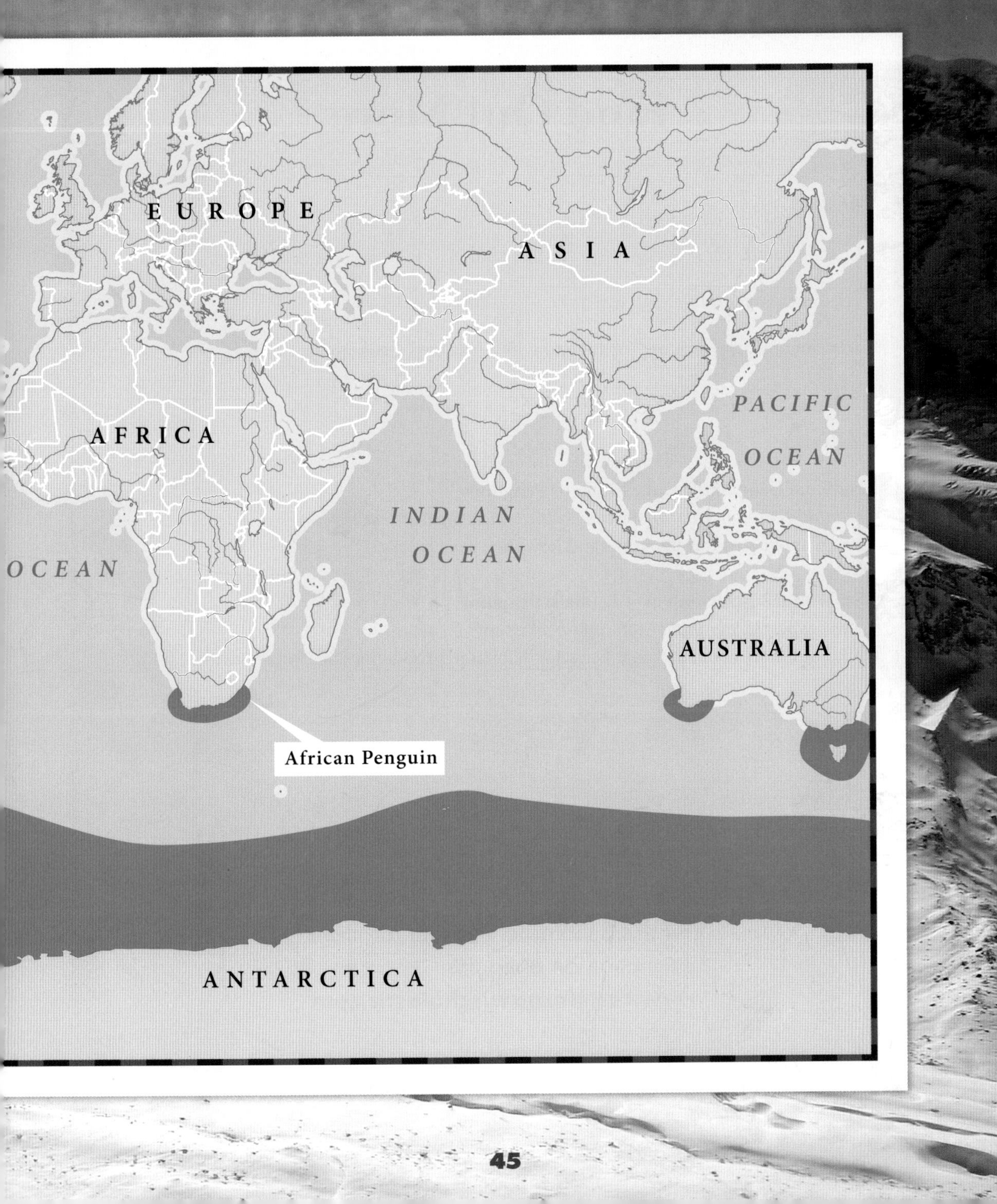
EUROPE
ASIA
PACIFIC
OCEAN
AFRICA
INDIAN
OCEAN
OCEAN
AUSTRALIA
African Penguin
ANTARCTICA

Find Out More

Books

Cussen, Sarah. *Those Perky Penguins.* Sarasota, FL: Pineapple Press, 2011.

Friedman, Mel. *Antarctica.* New York: Children's Press, 2009.

Schreiber, Anne. *Penguins!* Washington, DC: National Geographic, 2009.

Web Sites

National Geographic Kids: Emperor Penguins
http://kids.nationalgeographic.com/kids/animals/creaturefeature/emperor-penguin
Learn about emperor penguins and how they have chicks.

SeaWorld/Busch Gardens—Animals: Penguins
www.seaworld.org/animal-info/info-books/penguin/index.htm
Find out more about penguin behavior, habitat, reproduction, and conservation.

Visit this Scholastic web site for more information on penguins:
www.factsfornow.scholastic.com

Index

(Index continued)

About the Author

Lucia Raatma earned a bachelor's degree from the University of South Carolina and a master's degree from New York University. She has authored dozens of books for young readers, and she particularly enjoys writing about wildlife and conservation. She and her family enjoy visiting the African penguins at the local zoo. For more information, visit *www.luciaraatma.com*